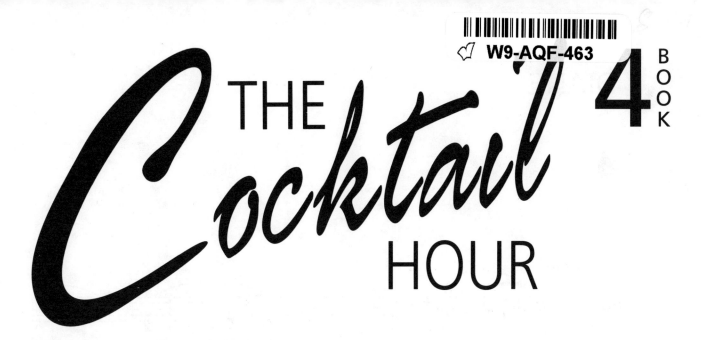

THE Cocktail HOUR

BOOK 4

Edited by PETER FOSS
Cover design: Headline Publicity
First Published as Velvet Touch Book Four 1986. This Edition 1992
© International Music Publications

International Music Publications
Southend Road, Woodford Green,
Essex IG8 8HN, England.
ISBN 0 86359 360 7

215-2-235

DIANE

Words and Music by
ERNO RAPEE and LEW POLLACK

CAN'T HELP LOVIN' DAT MAN

Words by OSCAR HAMMERSTEIN II
Music by JEROME KERN

DON'T CRY OUT LOUD

Words and Music by
CAROLE BAYER SAGER and PETER ALLEN

HARBOUR LIGHTS

Words and Music by
JIMMY KENNEDY and HUGH WILLIAMS

THE HEATHER ON THE HILL

Words by ALAN JAY LERNER
Music by FREDERICK LOEWE

HEAVEN (Theme from Highway To Heaven)

By DAVID ROSE

HOW TO HANDLE A WOMAN

Words by ALAN JAY LERNER
Music by FREDERICK LOEWE

HOW DEEP IS YOUR LOVE

Words and Music by
BARRY, ROBIN and MAURICE GIBB

IF YOU LOVE ME (Hymne A L'Amour)

English Lyrics by GEOFFREY PARSONS
French Words by EDITH PIAF
Music by MARGUERITE MONNOT

38

I'LL GET BY (As Long As I Have You)

Words by ROY TURK
Music by FRED AHLERT

I MADE IT THROUGH THE RAIN

Words by DRAY SHEPPERD, BRUCE SUSSMAN,
JACK FELDMAN and BARRY MANILOW
Music by GERARD KENNY

I'M CONFESSIN' (That I Love You)

Words by AL J NEIBURG
Music by DOC DAUGHERTY and ELLIS REYNOLDS

I ONLY HAVE EYES FOR YOU

Words by AL DUBIN
Music by HARRY WARREN

I'LL STRING ALONG WITH YOU

Words by AL DUBIN
Music by HARRY WARREN

LITTLE GREEN APPLES

Words and Music
by BOBBY RUSSELL

MAY EACH DAY

Words by MORT GREEN
Music by GEORGE WYLE

MY PRAYER (Avant De Mourir)

English Lyrics by JIMMY KENNEDY
Music by GEORGES BOULANGER

THE OLD FASHIONED WAY

English Lyrics by AL KASHA and JOEL HIRSCHHORN
Original Words by CHARLES AZNAVOUR
Music by GEORGES GARVARENTZ

PARADISE

Words by NACIO HERB BROWN and GORDON CLIFFORD
Music by NACIO HERB BROWN

RAINING IN MY HEART

Words and Music by
BOUDLEAUX BRYANT and FELICE BRYANT

86

SUMMERTIME

Words by DuBOSE HEYWARD
Music by GEORGE GERSHWIN

SMOKE GETS IN YOUR EYES

Words by OTTO HARBACH
Music by JEROME KERN

STELLA BY STARLIGHT

Words by NED WASHINGTON
Music by VICTOR YOUNG

SWEET AND LOVELY

Words and Music by GUS ARNHEIM,
HARRY TOBIAS and JULES LEMARE

THERE'S A SMALL HOTEL

Words by LORENZ HART
Music by RICHARD RODGERS

105

106

Printed in Great Britain by St Edmundsbury Press Ltd, Bury St Edmunds, Suffolk

THE Cocktail HOUR

CAN'T HELP LOVIN' DAT MAN

Verse

Oh listen, sister, I love my Mister man
   and I can't tell yo' why,
Dere ain't no reason why I should
   love dat man.
It must be sumpin' dat de angels done plan.
De chimbley's smokin', de roof is leakin' in,
But he don't seem to care,
He can be happy with jes' a sip of gin.
I even loves him when his kisses got gin.

Refrain

Fish got to swim and birds got to fly,
I got to love one man till I die,
Can't help lovin' dat man of mine.

Tell me he's lazy, tell me he's slow,
Tell me I'm crazy, may-be, I know,
Can't help lovin' dat man of mine.

When he goes away dat's a rainy day,
And when he comes back dat day is fine,
The sun will shine.

He can come home as late as can be,
Home without him ain't no home to me,
Can't help lovin' dat man of mine.

DIANE

"I'm in Heav'n when I see you smile,
Smile for me my Diane;
And though ev'rything's dark all the while,
I can see you Diane,
You have lighted the road leading home:
Pray for me when you can,
But no matter wherever I roam
Smile for me, my Diane".

DON'T CRY OUT LOUD

Baby cried the day the circus came to town,
   'cause she didn't like parades just passing by her.
So she painted on a smile and took up with some
   clown,
And she danced without a net up on the wire.
I know a lot about her 'cause you see,
Baby is an awful lot like me.

We don't dry out loud, we keep it inside,
   learn how to hide our feelings.
Fly high and proud and if you should fall
   remember you almost had it all.

Baby saw the day they pulled the big top down,
   they left behind her dreams among the litter.
And the different kind of love she thought she'd
   found,

Was nothing more than sawdust and some glitter.
But baby can't be broken 'cause you see,
She had the finest teacher, that's me.

I taught her don't cry out loud,
Just keep it inside, learn how to hide your feeling.
Fly high and proud and if you should fall
   remember you almost had it all.

Dont't cry out loud, keep it inside,
Learn how to hide your feelings.
Fly high and proud, and if you should fall
   remember you almost had it all.

Keep it inside, just learn how to hide your feelings.
Fly high and proud, and if you should fall
   remember you almost had it all.

                 (and fade)

HARBOUR LIGHTS

I saw the Harbour Lights,
They only told me we were parting,
The same old Harbour Lights,
That once brought you to me.

I watched the Harbour Lights,
How could I help if tears were starting?
Goodbye to tender nights,
Beside the silv'ry sea.

I longed to hold you near
   and kiss you just once more
But you were on the ship
   and I was on the shore

Now I know lonely nights,
For all the while my heart is whisp'ring,
Some other Harbour Lights
   will steal your love from me.

THE HEATHER ON THE HILL

The mist of May is in the gloamin';
   and all the clouds are holdin' still
So take my hand and let's go roamin'
   through the heather on the hill.

The mornin' dew is blinkin' yonder
   there's lazy music in the rill
And all I want to do is wander
   through the heather on the hill.

There may be other days as rich and rare
There may be other springs as full and fair
But they won't be the same
   they'll come and go
For this I know;
That when the mist is in the gloamin'
And all the clouds are holdin' still
If you're not there I won't go roamin'
   through the heather on the hill.
The heather on the hill.

HEAVEN
(Theme from Highway To Heaven)
— *Instrumental*

HOW DEEP IS YOUR LOVE

And when you rise in the morning sun
I feel you touch me in the pouring rain
And the moment that you wander far from me
I wanna feel you in my arms again.
When you come to me on a summer breeze,
Keep me warm in your love then you softly leave.
And it's me you need to show
   how deep is your love, is your love?
How deep is your love?
I really need to learn,
'Cause we're living in a world of fools
Breaking us down when they all should let us be.
We belong to you and me.
I believe in you.
You know the door to my barest soul.
You're the light in my deepest darkest hour.
You're my saviour when I fall
And you may not think that I care for you
When you know down inside that I really do
And it's me you need to show,
   how deep is your love, is your love?
How deep is your love?
I really need to learn
'Cause we're living in a world of fools
Breaking us down when they all should let us be.
We belong to you and me.
La la la la la la la la la la la la la la la
La la la la la la la la la
La la la la la la la la la la la la
When you come to me on a summer breeze
Keep me warm in your love then you softly leave.
And it's me you need to show
   how deep is your love, is your love?
How deep is your love?
I really need to learn,
'Cause we're living in a world of fools
Breaking us down when they all should let us be.
We belong to you and me.
La la la la la
How deep is your love, how deep is your love?
I really need to learn
'Cause we're living in a world of fools
Breaking us down when they all should let us be.

HOW TO HANDLE A WOMAN

How to handle a woman,
There's a way, said a wise old man
A way known by ev'ry woman
  since the whole rigmarole began.
"Do I flatter her?" I begged him answer.
"Do I threaten or cagole or plead?
Do I brood or play the gay romancer?"
Said he, smiling "No, indeed".
How to handle a woman,
Mark me well, I will tell you, sir.
The way to handle a woman is to love her,
Simply love her,
Merely love her, love her, love her!"

IF YOU LOVE ME

If the sun should tumble from the sky,
If the sea should suddenly run dry,
If you love me, really love me,
Let it happen I won't care.

If it seems that ev'rything is lost,
I will smile and never count the cost,
If you love me, really you love me,
Let it happen, darling, I won't care.

Shall I catch a shooting star?
Shall I bring it where you are?
If you want me to I will.
You can set me any task,
I'll do anything you ask,
If you'll only love me still

When atlast our life on earth is through,
I will share eternity with you,
If you love me, really love me,
Then whatever happens I won't care.

I'LL GET BY
(As Long As I Have You)

I'll get by as long as I have you,
Though there be rain and darkness too
I'll not complain, I'll see it through.
Though I/you may be far away it's true
Say, what care I, dear I'll get by
  as long as I have you.

I'LL STRING ALONG WITH YOU

You may not be an angel, 'Cause angesl are so few,
But until the day that one comes along,
I'll string along with you.

I'm looking for an angel to sing my love song to,
And until the day that one comes along,
I'll sing my song to you.

For ev'ry little fault that you have,
Say! I've got three or four,
The human little faults you do have,
Just make me love you more.

You may not be an angel,
  but still I'm sure you'll do,
So until the day that one comes along,
I'll string along with you.

I MADE IT THROUGH THE RAIN

We dreamers have our ways
  of facin' rainy days, and somehow we survive.
We keep the feelings warm,
  protect them from the storm until our time arrives.
Then one day the sun appears,
  and we come shining through those lonely years
I made it through the rain.
I kept my world protected.
I made it through the rain.
I kept my point of view.
I made it through the rain,
  and found myself respect by the others who
  got rain on too and made it through.
When friends are hard to find
  and life seems so unkind,
sometimes you feel afraid.
  sometimes you feel afraid.
Just aim beyond the clouds
  and rise above the crowds
  and start your own parade.
'Cause when I chased my fears away,
  that's when I knew that I could fin'lly say:
I made it through the rain.
I kept my world protected.
I made it through the rain.
I kept my point of view.
I made it through the rain,
  and found myself respected
  by the others who got rained on too
  and made it through.
I made it through the rain.
I kept my world protected.
I made it through the rain.
I kept my point of view.
I made it through the rain,
  and found myself respected
  by the others who got rained on too
  and made it through,
  and made it through.
I made it through.

I'M CONFESSIN' (THAT I LOVE YOU)

I'm confessin' that I love you;
Tell me, do you love me too?
I'm confessin that I need you, honest I do,
  need you ev'ry moment!

In your eyes I read such strange things,
But your lips deny they're true;
Will your answer really change things,
  making me blue?

I'm afraid, some day, you'll leave me, saying
  "Can't we still be friends?"
If you go, you know you'll grieve me,
  all in life on you depends,

Am I guessin' that you love me
  dreaming dreams of you in vain?
I'm confessin' that I love you, over again.

I ONLY HAVE EYES FOR YOU

Are the stars out tonight?
I don't know if it's cloudy or bright,
'Cause I only have eyes for you, dear

The moon may be high,
  but I can't see a thing in the sky,
'Cause I only have eyes for you.

I don't know if we're in a garden,
Or on a crowded avenue,

You are here, so am I
Maybe millions of people go by,
But they all disappear from view,
And I only have eyes for you.

LITTLE GREEN APPLES

And I wake up in the morning with my hair down
  in my eyes and she says, "Hi".
And I stumble to the breakfast table while
  the kids are going off to school, goodbye.
And she reaches out an' takes my hand squeezes
  it says "How you feelin' Hon."
And I look across at smiling lips that warm my
  heart and see my morning sun.
And if that's not lovin' me then all I've got to say.
God didn't make little green apples and it
  don't rain in Indianapolis in the summer time,
There's no such thing as Doctor Suess,
  Disneyland and Mother Goose is no
  nursery rhyme.
God didn't make little green apples and it don't
  rain in Indianapolis in the summertime,
And when my self is feeling low I think about
  her face aglow to ease my mind
Sometimes I call her up at home
  knowing she's busy
And ask if she could get away and meet me
  and grab a bite to eat
And she drops what she's doin' and hurries
  down to meet me and I'm always late.
But she sit's waiting patiently and smiles when
  she first sees me 'cause she's made that way.
And if that's not lovin's me then all I've got to say.
God didn't make little green apples and it don't
  snow in Minneapolis when the winter comes.
There's not such thing as make believe
  puppy dogs and autumn leaves and B.B. guns.
Good didn't make little green apples

(fade out)

MAY EACH DAY

May each day in the week be a good day.
May the Lord always watch over you
And may all of your hopes turn to wishes
And may all of your wishes come true.

May each day in the month be a good day.
May you make friends with each one you meet.
And may all of your day dreams be mem'ries
And may all of your mem'ries be sweet.

The weeks turn to months and the months
  turn into years.
There'll be sadness and joy.
There'll be laughter and tears.
But one thing I pray to heaven above
May each of your days be a day full of love.

May each day in the year be a good day.
May each dawn find you happy and gay
And may all of your days be as lovely
As the one you shared with me today.
May each day in your life be a good day
  and good night.

MY PRAYER

My prayer is to linger with you
At the end of the day in a dream that's divine
My prayer is a rapture in blue
With the world far away and your lips close to mine.
Tonight while our hearts are aglow
Oh, tell me the words that I'm longing to know.
My prayer and the answer you give
May they still be the same for as long as we live
That you'll always be there at the end of my prayer.

THE OLD FASHIONED WAY

Dance in the old fashioned way
Won't you stay in my arms?
Just melt against my skin
And let me feel your heart,
Don't let the music win by dancing far apart.
Come close where you belong,
Let's hear our secret song.
Dance in the old fashioned way
Won't you stay in my arms
And we'll discover highs we never knew before,
If we just close our eyes and dance around the floor,
That gay old fashioned way
That makes me love you more.

Dance in the old fashioned way
Won't you stay in my arms
And we'll discover highs we never knew before,
If we just close our eyes and dance around the floor,
That gay old fashioned way
That makes me love you more.

PARADISE

And then she/he holds my hand, Mm
Then Cupid takes command, Mm
Her/his eyes reveal a love that's real,
And the sweet smile I see brings heav'n to me!
And then her/his lips meet mine, Mm
With kisses so divine, Mm
Her/his love, each fond caress,
They lead the way to happiness,
She/he takes me to Paradise!

RAINING IN MY HEART

The sun is out, the sky is blue,
    there's not a cloud to spoil the view
But it's raining, raining in my heart.
The weatherman says, "Clear today",
    he doesn't know you've gone away
And it's raining, raining in my heart.
Oh, misery, misery, what's gonna become of me.
I tell my blues they mustn't show,
    but soon these tears are bound to flow
'Cause it's raining, raining in my heart.

SMOKE GETS IN YOUR EYES

They asked me how I knew my true love was true;
I of course replied, "Something here inside
    cannot be denied."
They said "someday you'll find,
    all who love are blind,
When your heart's on fire, you must realize
Smoke gets in your eyes".
So I chaffed them and I gaily laughed
    to think they could doubt my love.
Yet today my love has flown away
    I am without my love.
Now laughing friends deride tears I cannot hide.
So I smile and say "When a lovely flame dies,
Smoke gets in your eyes."

STELLA BY STARLIGHT

The song a robin sings
Through years of endless springs.
The murmur of a brook at eventide
That ripples by a nook where two lovers hide.
A great symphonic theme,
That's Stella by starlight and not a dream.
My heart and I agree
She's ev'rything on earth to me.

SUMMERTIME

Summertime an' the livin' is easy,
Fish are jumpin', and the cotton is high.
Oh, yo' daddy's rich, and yo' ma is good lookin',
So hush, little baby, don' you cry.

One of these mornin's you goin' to rise up singin',
Then you'll spread your wings an' you'll take the sky.
But till that mornin' there's a nothin' can harm you
With Daddy an' Mammy standin' by.

SWEET AND LOVELY

Sweet and lovely, sweeter than the roses in May
Sweet and lovely, heaven must have sent her my way.
Skies above me never were as blue as her eyes
And she loves me, who would want
    a sweeter surprise?
When she nestles in my arms so tenderly
There's a thrill that words cannot express,
In my heart a song of love is taunting me,
Melody haunting me
Sweet and lovely sweeter than the roses in May
And she loves me there is nothing more I can say.

THERE'S A SMALL HOTEL

There's a small hotel with a wishing well;
I wish that we were there together.
There's a bridal suite; one room bright and neat,
Complete for us to share together.
Looking through the window you can see
    a distant steeple;
Not a sign of people, who wants people?
When the steeple bell says, "Goodnight, sleep well"
We'll thank the small hotel together.

(Repeat)

We"ll creep into our little shell
And we will thank the small hotel together.